THE ANXIOUS ELEPHANT

A CHILDREN'S BOOK ABOUT OVERTHINKING, BEING REALISTIC, AND MANAGING YOUR EMOTIONS

WRITTEN BY
CHARLOTTE DANE

ILLUSTRATED BY
ADAM RIONG

THE ANXIOUS ELEPHANT

Elephant would always keep his calm and think, "It's not as bad as it seems!" He would never fell into the trap of anxious thoughts creating even more anxious thoughts!

When Elephant participated in a polo tournament, he thought he would be the worst player on his team.

But then he remembered that he had practiced for 20 hours a week and scored the winning goal in last year's tournament. And you know what? After calming down, he did the same this year, too!

One time Elephant was in a play and forgot his lines! Oh no! He thought everyone would laugh at him for the entire year.

But soon he realized that no one cared, or even noticed that there was anything wrong. No problem!

And just last week, Elephant's friend Fennec Fox misspelled Elephant's name in class.

Instead of thinking that Fennec Fox hated him, he rememebered that Fennec Fox was terrible at spelling!

Elephant's friends started avoiding him because his anxiety made them anxious as well.

One day, Fox saw Elephant sitting alone.

Fox asked Elephant why he was crying. Elephant replied, "Whenever something bad happens, I can't control where my thoughts go!"

"Something I do to beat anxiety and remain calm is called the Truth Exercise. It's great for finding the difference between your thoughts, emotions, and what is really happening. It can help you understand if your worries are actually true!"

"Second, ask yourself what evidence you have for your anxious thought. You probably won't find any. Third, ask yourself how one of your friends would react to your anxious thought. They probably wouldn't be very worried!"

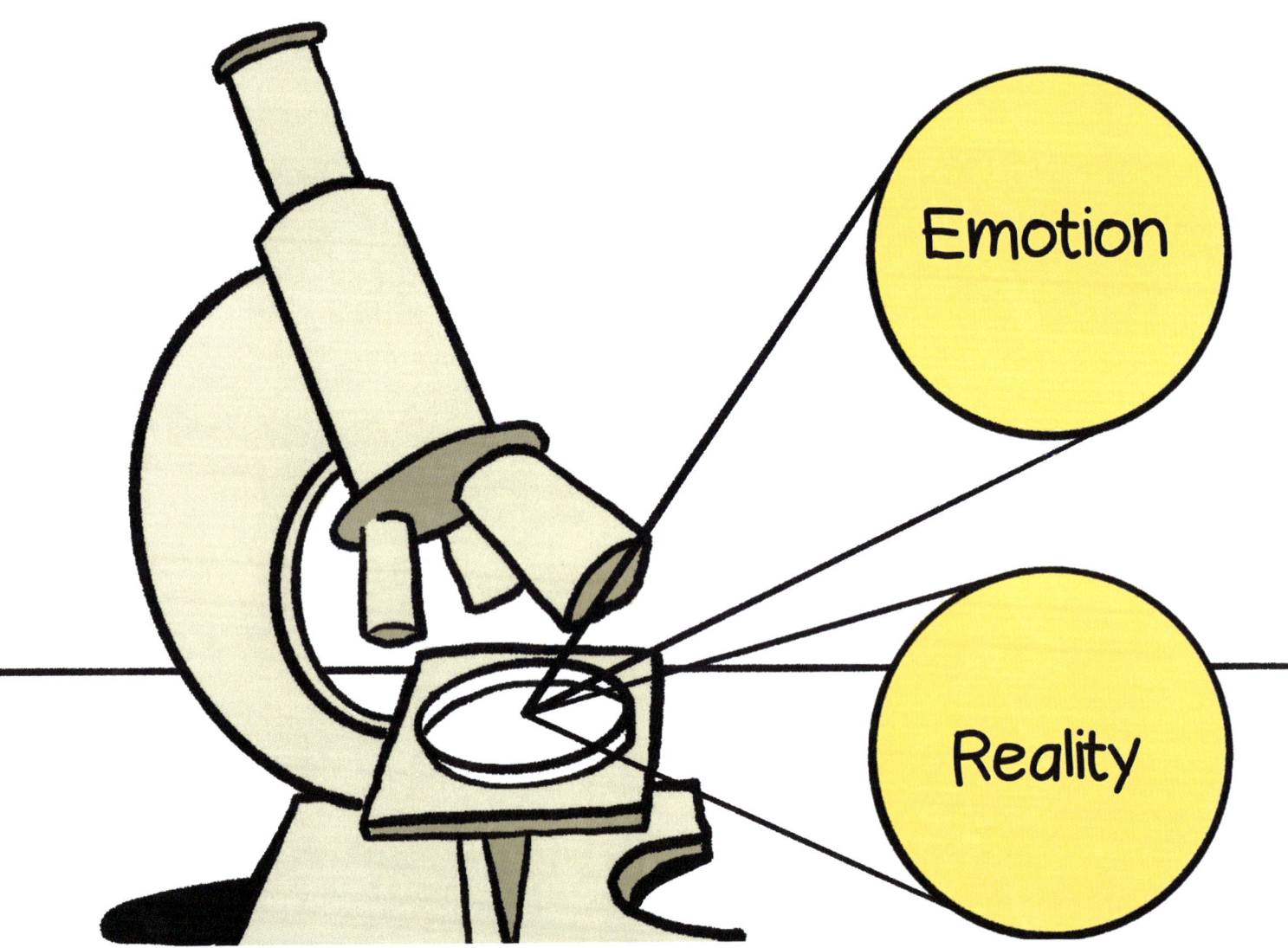

"The Truth Exercise lets us see that life always balances the good and bad!"

The next week, Elephant was anxious about completing a big project on time. Instead of thinking that he would fail, he used the Truth Exercise!

(1) Was it true that he would definitely fail?
No!

(2) What was the evidence that he would fail?
None!

(3) What would a friend think?
That if Elephant focused, he would be just fine! So go!
Elephant relaxed and could finish the task at hand.

Elephant tried the Truth Exercise again when he got into a fight with Penguin. He was worried that their friendship was over.

The Truth Exercise can help you, too. All you need to do is slow down and realize that the real world is different from how you feel about it, and you can prove this to yourself and get rid of all your anxiety easily.

Printed in Great Britain
by Amazon